P re-

To Do

List

A trusted guide for families preparing for the college application and scholarship process!

BIO

Khalilah Hall is the Owner and Chief Planning Officer of The Planner, LLC which provides College and Scholarship Help services. Her focus is helping families successfully navigate the college process and finding collegiate financial assistance and scholarships. She has helped hundreds of families navigate this process and take advantage of college savings opportunities since 2010.

Armed with 20 years of experience of helping consumers make financial decisions for their families, Hall first applied her organization and communication skills to the education arena when her eldest child began her own college search. After much research and many scholarship applications, Hall's daughter received over $30,000 in scholarships and graduated from the University of Central Florida with no out-of-pocket cost to her family.

Hall desires for this success to be duplicated for the families that she assists. In addition to working one on one with students and families to create a personal college strategy plan, Hall also facilitates workshops and webinars on various topics ranging from college admissions, essays, organization and applying for scholarships, to name a few.

Hall has partnered with non-profits, community organizations and schools to facilitate workshops for their students. She has also been a featured panelist at multi-city conferences, such as the PowHERful summits hosted by award winning journalist, Soledad O'Brien. Hall prides herself on developing personable relationships with her clients which continues into their post graduate years, by providing career advice and mentoring them for success in the workplace.

"The vision of this book is part of the mission of this great author. It is a hope that parents and students take away great knowledge surrounding college preparedness!"

-Erica A., Financial Aid Consultant, Univ. of Florida

Introduction

Congratulations on deciding to pursue a college education!

This is a huge and honorable step towards your future. While it can be a very tedious, lengthy and sometimes confusing process, it's not insurmountable.

Planning and preparing for the college application and scholarship process, starts well before a student reaches the twelfth grade. Conversations about college typically start in middle school or junior high.

There are parents who attend my workshops and webinars, whose children are in the 7th or 8th grade. Why do they attend? Because they prefer to get a head start and learn about the process early. I commend them!

Some parents may say, "I have a LOT of time before worrying about college."

Have you noticed how quickly time passes?

While a 7th or 8th grader may have a few years before they begin submitting college applications, it's never too early to start discussing potential careers.

I can't believe that I have another high-schooler! So, trust me, time can go by fast. We're in the throngs of the college process, but I'm ready! I'm using this same information and tips that I'm sharing in this book with YOU.

When you feel overwhelmed, refer to the pages of this book. This book will be a great guide for you, through the college application and scholarship process.

Contents

Parents, being that you're an integral piece of this process, I've included tips for YOU. Look for the Parent Tip at the end of each chapter. These tips are based on my personal experience.

Help! Where do I start?

First things first, let's talk grades.

As a carpenter builds a solid foundation for a home, the same applies to a high school student aspiring to attend college. Your grades are the solid foundation for which any college acceptance and/or scholarships will be awarded.

Building a relationship with your guidance counselor is critical. They have a wealth of knowledge and connections in their network that will prove to be beneficial in your pursuit of a college education. Be sure to confirm with your school guidance counselor that you're on track to satisfy all course requirements needed for graduation.

When deciding what field you're interested in studying or the college you want to attend, your counselor will be eager to help you explore your options. Also, if/when you need a letter of recommendation, guess who should be at the top of your list? You guessed it. Your guidance counselor!

We'll discuss letters of recommendation later in the book; however, it's important to note that a letter of recommendation from your guidance counselor carries a lot of weight. Many students often overlook the option of asking their counselors. Don't let that be you! ASK.

This is an exciting time, with many senior activities, graduation pictures, college tours, etc taking place. It's ok to enjoy this time, but do not let your grades suffer at the hands of 'fun'.

While your GPA from the end of your 11th grade year will be used for college applications, an updated transcript will need to be sent during your 12th grade year. Therefore, do not risk your chances of being waitlisted or denied admission because your grades and GPA dropped.

Each college has their own requirements in regards to the minimum GPA to be accepted. However, the universal pre-requisite that you cannot bypass, is the need to have 'good' grades.

Not every student will have a 4.0 or greater GPA; however, applying for college is a very competitive process. Therefore, having a high GPA works in your favor. Your GPA is one of the first pieces of information, that the admissions team will check. Therefore, doing your best and obtaining the highest grades possible is HIGHLY recommended. Also, consider taking challenging courses such as Advanced Placement and Honors courses. This looks great on your transcript.

All students have a "dream college" they would love to attend. How did you compile your list of 20 colleges? Don't worry, every student has their own method of deciding what college should garner a spot on their *list*.

Creating this list should be an exciting process for both the student and their parent/ family. Especially when there's a family legacy of attending a certain college. However, the pressure of deciding whether to keep with family tradition or attend a different school can be a challenge. For those who do not have that pressure, narrowing down your list of schools can still be a feat.

When my daughter compiled her list of prospective colleges, I encouraged her to reach out to alumni of the school, to get their opinion and hear their experiences. In this age of social media, this is extremely easy. One way is to search hashtags (#)

related to the college. You can derive a lot about the culture of a school by searching social media. Use caution of course, because you can't *fully* judge a school simply by a tweet or post.

Let's discuss how you can narrow down your choices to a manageable number of schools that appear to be a good fit. Here are a few important questions you'll want to consider:

1. Does the college offer a degree in the field I want to study?
2. Is my GPA and test scores within the minimum range accepted?
3. Can I afford the cost of tuition?
4. What percentage of students receive financial aid (other than loans)?
5. Does the college offer non-need based aid?
6. If the college is outside of my town, city or state, am I comfortable with being away from family?
7. How far away from home do I want to be? If I need to get back home for an emergency, will I have the transportation or funds needed to get home quickly?

8. If you have a car, are freshmen allowed to drive? If not, is this a 'deal breaker'?
9. Is on campus housing available?
10. Are freshmen required to stay on campus?
11. Do they have the sports, fraternities, sororities or other student clubs that I'm interested in?

*This is not an all-inclusive list. There are other factors you should consider when selecting a college. At the end of this chapter is a copy of my Prospective College Checklist. Visit my website www.collegeandscholarshiphelp.com to download a copy of the *Prospective College Checklist*.

Before we move on to applications, let's discuss **target, reach and safety** schools. You've likely heard of these terms and may be confused on what they mean.

- Your **reach** school is one where you're lacking in a few areas such as a low GPA or ACT/ SAT scores. This school may be in the top 10 on your list, but there are gaps that need to be addressed asap. Don't be discouraged about applying, only the admissions team can decide whether you'll be accepted or not. Continue working on increasing your GPA & test scores.

- Your *safety* school is one that you currently exceed the GPA and test score standards. This school may not be on your top 10 list, but it could be a good fit. Be careful not to discard these schools because they're not in the top 10 on your list. They may actually be a good fit and offer you merit aid!
- Your *target* school is one that you currently meet or exceed the minimum GPA and test scores. You really, really like the school and it's in the top 5 on your list.

Parent Tip:

- *Be involved in the process, use the free checklist I mentioned on the previous page to help with the decision-making process.*

- *When researching prospective colleges, you can learn a lot about the culture and student experience by connecting with alumni of the school. They will often be eager to share their experiences (good and bad). This could also be a valuable connection for your student's network.*

You'll find that the alumni typically offer scholarships. Having a letter of recommendation from a respected alumnus, can be the deciding factor for a scholarship! This is not 100% guaranteed, but the possibility is there.

NOTES

<u>NOTES</u>

NOTES

Applications and Admissions

College applications, scholarship applications, job applications. Applications, applications, applications. You can't bypass them, but you don't have to dread them!

Let's discuss the different types of college admissions.

The most common type of admission is the *regular* admissions cycle which refers to the college/ university having a specific deadline. This date is typically in late fall or early winter. All applications are reviewed and admission decisions are made at one time.

Some colleges will have *rolling* admissions, where they accept applications year-round, until all spots for the next term are filled. Rolling admissions are made on a first come, first serve basis..

Open admissions are typically offered by online colleges and/or community colleges. Any applicant who has a diploma or GED (General Educational Development) are *typically* admitted. *This may vary.*

Early decision is an option some students will exercise when they are 100% sure that the college they're applying to is there top and only choice. If you exercise this option and are accepted, keep in mind that you are bound to this school and <u>must</u> withdraw any other offers of acceptance. You should also be comfortable with paying the full cost of attendance, if needed, since financial aid packages typically aren't determined before you receive your Early Decision acceptance letter.

Early action is similar to early decision; however, it's not binding. If you apply early and are accepted, you can make a decision at that time or wait until spring to notify the college of your decision.

Just like there are various types of admissions, this is true for applications as well.

Colleges have the option of using a **universal application** or their own private application. The **common application** is widely known.

What are the benefits of using the *Common Application*? You can apply to multiple colleges and universities, using ONE application. This is a very convenient process. However, not all schools accept the Common Application. You'll need to check the college website or call and confirm if the college uses this application.

While many schools accept the Common Application, some may also require students to complete their private application. This can result in two application fees and additional time needed to complete BOTH.

I remember when my daughter applied to multiple schools. She was accepted into her top 3 choices, waitlisted for one and deferred for spring term at another.

She ultimately decided to attend The University of Central Florida, which was one of her top choices.

This was a great decision because it wasn't far, but also not too close to feel as if she's still at home. The application fee was $30. However, application fees <u>vary</u> and can range upwards of $50+, depending on the college or university.

Be sure to speak with your guidance counselor or the college admissions office about application waivers. You may qualify for a waiver. My motto is, "If you don't ask, you'll never know".

Speaking of waivers, did you know that waivers are available for both the SAT & ACT tests? Yes! This is another task for your 'to do list'. Check with your guidance counselor to see if you're eligible.

I've heard many students ask, "Which test is better or easier?" There is no clear-cut answer. It's based on the individual student. Both tests are offered multiple times a year and you can find more information on the SAT by visiting The College Board website. Information on the ACT test can be found by visiting ACT.org Take each test a few times and then you can decide which test you like the best.

Important Application Tips:

- Read the application thoroughly! Do not skip a section.

- Call the college if you have ANY questions. Don't assume their intent.

- Make yourself known to the Admissions office staff. *(In a good way of course)* Advisors <u>want</u> prospective students to call and inquire. This is an opportunity to make connections!

- Complete the entire application and be sure to click SUBMIT! Admission Advisors have told me countless stories of how students will complete the application, save and exit the portal, but forget to go back in and SUBMIT the application. As a result, they are never considered for admission. Don't let this be you.

- Submit the essay on time, do not miss the deadline! If it requires mailing, target to have it in the mail, no later than 5 days before the actual due date.

- Have 2-3 people review and proofread your application. This extra step will help ensure that you're presenting your *best self*.
- Each college should have a freshman profile posted on their website, which shows the GPA, test scores, etc. of the average freshman they accept. Keep in mind that the information shown may either be the <u>average</u> or the <u>minimum</u> and should be used as a reference only.

- Some colleges may be test optional, which means that you have the option to submit your SAT/ ACT scores for consideration during the admissions review process. If you do not submit your test scores, they will evaluate you based on your transcript. However, if you submit your test scores, they will be evaluated.

Parent Tip:

- *Some programs at the college may have a separate application and different deadline than the general college application deadline.*

Have your student confirm if the college of nursing or engineering for example, has a different deadline. Many students will apply to the school before the general deadline, but miss the application deadline for their specific program of interest.

- *If your student is interested in attending a college outside your area, call and inquire if they will be participating in a college fair or event near you. If so, some colleges will waive the application fee for students who attend that special event.*

- *You are the best advocate for your student. Be diligent in discovering if the college(s) are a good fit. Ask questions.*

NOTES

NOTES

FREE MONEY, is there really such a thing?

Now that you've compiled your list of colleges, researched the types of applications and confirmed deadlines, it's time to discuss the COST. Yes, the big, shiny penny. Correction... the mighty DOLLAR!

It's no surprise that the cost of college continues to rise. This can be a challenge for many families. With so many factors surrounding the pre-college process, when a child decides to attend college it's not just an individual decision, it's a family decision.

Whether a student chooses to attend college in their hometown, in-state, out-of-state or in another country, there are several cost factors to evaluate. We've discussed the application fees, but there are other fees such as tuition, books, housing, meal plans, etc. The total for these costs will vary depending on the college.

Generally, your costs will be lower if you attend a local college and stay at home. If you choose an in-state college, but outside of your home town and stay off campus, you should anticipate your expenses being higher.

Many students desire to attend college out-of-state. This is a great opportunity. However, keep in mind that costs *could* be higher than an in-state school.

I encourage all students to explore their options: Public vs. Private; In-state vs. Out-of-state; Study abroad; Community vs. Career School, there are many choices and the associated costs will vary.

There is a cost associated with every college. Most colleges will have several types of financial aid they offer students. In addition to Federal Student Aid which is determined using the data from your FAFSA (Free Application for Federal Student Aid), there are scholarships, loans, institutional grants, etc. Research ALL available options, and make note of HOW to qualify and WHEN to apply!

You may be familiar with the FAFSA and the Office of Federal Student Aid. If not, according to studentaid.ed.gov, Federal Student Aid is part of the U.S. Department of Education. They provide more than $120 billion in federal student aid to help pay for college or career school.

When you complete the FAFSA, you are submitting your information to the Office of Federal Student

Aid. The FAFSA application can be found at www.fafsa.ed.gov They review your application and determine your EFC (expected family contribution).

The final cost of how much you'll have to pay for college, is determined after the college receives your information from the Office of Federal Student Aid and evaluates you for any Pell Grants, work study, loans, scholarships, Merit Aid and/or institutional grants. After you receive an acceptance letter, you can expect the college to advise shortly thereafter, how much financial aid you'll be awarded.

Types of Financial Aid (not all inclusive)

- **Pell Grants**
  - *Money the federal government gives students to help pay for college*
  - *Federally funded*
  - *Amounts vary per academic year*
  - *There may be more than one type of federal grant available, check with the college to confirm*

- **Work study**
  - *Provides part-time student employment to help cover education expenses*
  - *Federally funded*

- Very competitive and every student may not receive work study

- **Loans** (*amount varies per loan option*)
  - Money that is borrowed and expected to be repaid with interest
  - *Subsidized – Need based*
  - *Unsubsidized – Non-need based*
  - *Parent Plus – Used by parents to cover their child(ren) education costs*
  - *Private loans – Offered by lending institutions (banks, credit unions, etc)*

SCHOLARSHIPS = FREE money!

Where is it? How do I apply? When do I apply?

Did you know that <u>billions</u> of dollars that are specifically donated for scholarships go unclaimed? Yes! Unfortunately.

I recently had a conversation with a Financial Aid Advisor who shared that there were a large number of scholarships offered by the college. The scholarships are often listed on the college's financial aid page and specifies the requirements; however, students do not apply, even though there are several who <u>qualify</u>.

How is that so, you may ask?

It's not that the students cannot use the additional funds. The feedback the financial aid office receives is that the student does not want to write an essay.

Let's face it, most scholarships will require an essay. The essay allows the donor to learn more about your goals, and any obstacles you've overcame. Writing a 500 or 1,000-word essay can be the determining factor for if you're awarded a scholarship.

Imagine that you're awarded a $5,000 scholarship after submitting a 500-word essay which took 4 hours to write. That equates to $1,250 per hour! Not many high school students earn $1,250 per hour.

During my workshops, I discuss the importance of having a generic essay on hand at all times. You will find that many scholarships will ask applicants to write about their goals or how they overcame obstacles. Having a generic essay already completed makes it much easier to tweak AND quicker for you to apply.

After many applications, essays, letters of recommendations, trips to the post office, etc., my daughter received over $30,000 in scholarships, which covered all of her education at The University of Central Florida!

We are often asked, "How, did you do it?"

It required a LOT of online research, reaching out to my network and inquiring about scholarships. We stayed in constant contact with the college and checked their website for any new scholarships.

You'll notice that some colleges will offer a large number of alumni scholarships. This could be a result of very generous alumni who love to give back to their alma mater. Some colleges will also have endowments, which also funds scholarships.

Below is a list of organizations I found that offers scholarships. Feel free to search for these organizations or similar organizations in your area.

If you find that an organization does not offer a scholarship, ASK. Providing a scholarship *could* be a tax write off for a business.

As a bonus for purchasing this book, I'd like to send you a tool kit which includes a prospective college checklist, college application tracker, scholarship tracker and a student resume template! Send an email to info@collegandscholarshiphelp.com and put TOOLKIT in the subject line.

Organizations

- *Rotary Clubs*
- *Fraternities and Sororities*
- *Your parent's employer*
- *Religious Organizations (churches, synagogues, mosques, etc.)*
- *Your grandparents, aunts and uncle's employers*
- *Associations for the field you want to study (ie. Medical associations)*
- *Girl Scouts and Boy Scouts (YES, they have scholarships)*

Parent Tip:

- *Create a separate email address when registering for different scholarship sites. Expect to receive a LOT of emails. Having a separate email address will eliminate the overcrowding of your primary email account. It will also help you stay organized by sending everything college related to ONE email address.*

<u>NOTES</u>

NOTES

A Good essay or an Impeccable essay? Your choice.

The essay. The part of your overall application, besides your GPA and test scores, that carry a LOT of weight. Most students and parents really dread the essay portion of the application. This is understandable when you don't have a plan or can't think of what to include or not include.

Here's a few tips to help you compose your essay:

Tip #1: If given a choice, write your essay on a topic that resonates with you the most.

Tip #2: ATQ! Answer the Question. Don't over complicate the essay requirement.

Tip #3: Use your resume of accomplishments to help fill in the details of your paragraphs. *We'll discuss this more in the next chapter.

Tip #4: Don't stress when your first draft is not "perfect". You won't use your first draft as the final version.

Tip #5: Proofread, proofread, proofread. Have at least 2 other people read your essay. Preferably, one of them should be someone who offers a proofreading service such as myself. Or you can ask a teacher.

However, with the number of requests teachers receive, this may be a challenge. If you plan on using this as an option, plan to ask <u>at least 3 weeks</u> before you need it.

Tip #6: Stay within the word count or character count guidelines. Pay close attention to the instructions. Do not assume that the essay is 1,000 words. Some applications will state characters, so be careful.

Tip #7: <u>CRITICALLY IMPORTANT</u>: While it may be tempting for a parent to write their student's essay, please do not do this. Scholarship committees and admission advisors read thousands upon thousands of essays and they will IMMEDIATELY know when an adult has written the essay.

The essay must be in the voice of the student. There are several consultants and businesses that offer to write your essay. I caution you to try and refrain from using this type of service…. refer to tip #7.

Parent Tip:

Parents, trust me, I KNOW how hard and tempting it is to want to write the essay or pay someone to write it. However, it's not worth the risk of your student being disqualified from <u>thousands</u> of scholarship dollars or denied college admission.

I have heard many stories from Admissions Advisors on how a student was a great fit for the school, but they had grammatical errors and…. you guessed it, they KNEW the student didn't write the essay because it wasn't in the voice of a high school student.

Parents, your consolation prize is that you can proofread and suggest edits. Remember, it's a team effort and you both win in the end.

NOTES

To boast or not to boast? Your student resume.

A student resume and student profile are in essence the same document. Having a comprehensive and well thought out resume is <u>vital</u> to the college application and scholarship process.

Similar to how a job-seeker uses a resume to get their "foot in the door", your resume works the same, but from a college perspective.

Your resume is a tool to capture your most important skills, achievements, awards, etc. The resume gives the admissions and scholarship committee a view of what you've accomplished. In this very competitive process of applying to college, and vying for thousands of scholarship dollars, having a comprehensive resume is not merely an option, it's a requirement.

Most applications provide 3-4 lines, which is not enough space to capture ALL of your accomplishments. While some colleges may not require a resume with your application, I encourage students to submit one.

In some cases, your resume could be the deciding factor as to whether you're accepted or selected as the scholarship winner. With that said, be selective on what you include. Be strategic on what you include. If your desire is to become a doctor, be sure to include any medical related volunteer experience. If you desire to be the CEO of a non-profit, include examples of how you volunteered and fundraised for charities.

Also, include any student clubs or leadership roles you've held, even babysitting. This will demonstrate your ability to lead, make an impact and care for others. Colleges <u>want</u> students who are involved and well-rounded. They want you to bring that same passion and goodwill to their school. Your resume is YOUR opportunity to stand out from the rest!

NOTES

It's who you know!

Almost every scholarship will require <u>at least</u> one letter of recommendation. I've seen some scholarships that require three or four.

A letter of recommendation allows the reader to get to know you through a lens other than your application, resume or essay. There's a saying, "word of mouth is the best form of advertisement", which I agree with. It's important to think of your letters of recommendation as a "form of advertisement". We all want GOOD advertisement, right?

If you've attended one of my workshops or follow me on any social media platforms, you know that I emphasize the importance of having a resume/ student profile.

Some of you may be asking, "Why?"

Imagine a student who's been very active with school activities and volunteering in the community. A student who has won numerous award. A student who started his/ her own non-profit. The list can go on and on. However, it would be difficult and rather frustrating for that student, who has done all of these wonderful things, to remember ALL of this in their senior year.

Having a resume/ student profile, that you update every year is a *life-saver*! And I don't mean the candy.

When you're making your list of who you want to write a letter of recommendation, be sure to consider each of the below tips.

The most important tip is to only request letters of recommendation from individuals who will speak <u>favorably of you</u>.

This is not the time when you want someone who you've had a not so pleasant relationship with, to write a letter to a prospective donor or an admissions advisor. Seriously, letters of recommendation can be the deciding factor on if you're offered admission or selected as a scholarship winner.

Also, you should already have a great relationship with these individuals. When asking for letters of recommendation, I encouraged my daughter to start building relationships early, so when it was time to ask for a letter of recommendation, it wasn't awkward and the individual knew enough about her to write a great letter.

These tips will be helpful as you prepare to ask for a recommendation.

- Make sure it's someone who will speak favorably of you.

- Consider asking your teacher, guidance counselor, coach, pastor, club leader, well known business owner in your community, the CEO of a non-profit, etc.

- Ask the individual in person or over the phone, not via email. This is a personable request and the person you're asking should be able to hear WHY you chose them and WHY their recommendation is important.

- Ask for the letter at least 4 weeks before you need it. Give the individual(s) as much time as possible.

- Ask for the letter to be typed on their letterhead. When donors or advisors see a letterhead, it immediately implies professionalism.

- Ask the writer to print multiple copies. This is important, especially if you plan to apply to numerous colleges or scholarships.

- Ask them to save the letter in a PDF format and email it to you. So, you'll have it at all times and can print as many as you need.

- **IMPORTANT TIP**: Be sure they know your plan to use it more than once. If they receive a lot of phone calls from donors or colleges confirming their recommendation, they're not blindsided. Ask that they address the letter to "Whom it may concern".

- When you print it, use a heavy weight paper versus the standard copy paper. You can find this paper at your local office supply store for a fairly reasonable price. You want your letter to not only sound and look great, but feel great as well. Remember, everything you present reflects YOU!

NOTES

NOTES

Your community and WHY it's important

"Service to others is the rent you pay for your room here on earth." –
Muhammad Ali

Today, there are numerous charitable organizations and non-profits. With the increasing demand for basic needs, non-urgent medical care, disaster relief, etc there is an abundance of volunteer options to choose from.

There are many students who are active in their communities and have chosen to create their own non-profits, to support a cause that's meaningful to them. These organizations support efforts such as human rights, protecting the environment, feeding the homeless, animal welfare, etc.

Did you know there are scholarships where the main requirement is demonstrated community service? Why yes!

Before graduating high school, my daughter completed over 300 hours of community service. Several of the scholarships she won, was because of her community service. *These hours were completed 9th - 12th grade.

Parents often ask, "Will volunteering at multiple organizations look good on their student's profile or resume?" I recommend quality over quantity. While there's not a hard rule or limit on the number of organizations a student can volunteer at, choosing two or three organizations and consistently volunteering there, allows the student to build valuable relationships.

Remember those letters of recommendations? These relationships are great opportunities to secure recommendations.

After consistently volunteering at a local non-profit, the CEO wrote several letters of recommendation for my daughter's applications. I'm confident that those letters played a major role in her being selected for <u>many</u> scholarships.

Don't delay, get involved and make an impact in your local community!

NOTES

Papers are everywhere! How do I stay organized?

I remember having applications spread across the kitchen table. We had deemed that area as the "application zone". Applications, essays, letters of recommendation, to-do lists, post it notes, etc. Does this describe your kitchen table right now? If so, you are not alone. There are thousands of families who can attest to this being their current situation.

You may be an organized person for the most part, but going through the college and scholarship process can definitely push your limits. The last thing you want to occur, is to mail an application to the wrong address or send an essay to the wrong scholarship donor. You may think, "How could that happen?"

Oh, this HAS happened. Trust me.

While it may seem rare, trust me, I've had a few close encounters! If you plan to apply for multiple scholarships, such as 20 or more, in addition to your 10+ colleges, it's <u>critically important</u> to stay organized.

As you go through this process, you'll develop a system that works for you. However, if you need a little help getting started, I've created a tracker that you can download from my website www.collegeandscholarshiphelp.com

I used this tracker daily when my daughter applied to colleges, scholarships, requested letters of recommendation, etc. With so many items due and often they were due on the same day, having this tracker on hand was a tremendous stress reliever. I admit, it's very easy to get disorganized and place things in folders and forget where you placed them.

I remember preparing to mail 5 or so scholarship applications and sealed each envelope, only to have to reopen each one, because I couldn't remember which address label went on which envelope. This resulted in discarding the envelopes and taking additional time.

You may be wondering, "Why did she discard the envelope?" Because we wanted to present her <u>best self</u> to the committee.

Avoid sending torn or opened envelopes that have been sealed with tape. While it may seem minor, remember, this reflects YOU. Take pride in what you send, presentation matters.

In the next chapter, I'll introduce you to your new "best friend". This is a life saver, and again, I don't mean the candy.

You'll find a list of items that I personally used, in addition to the tracker. Remember, organization is key!

Parent Tip:

- *Allow your student to populate the tracker for each college and/or scholarship they apply for. This allows them to be involved and more invested in the process. Seeing what's required to stay organized should help them understand why you've asked 3 times if they have the letter of recommendation from their coach.*

- *It's ok to review and check the tracker afterwards, to ensure nothing is missing.*

- *If you develop a system that works for you, by all means use it. The key is to stay organized!*

NOTES

Your new "Best Friend"

There were many instances of when I found out about a scholarship that was due the same day or the next day. If it had to be postmarked that day, I didn't have time to go home and print her essay. Therefore, I had her print several copies and place it in the binder, my BEST-FRIEND during the process! Trust me, this is one 'best friend' that you'll want to keep by your side at all times.

I recall several people asking me why I always had the binder with me. After I explained what it was for, those same individuals would stop me in the hallway or call to tell me about a scholarship they came across!

Here's what you'll need:

- A 3-ring binder. Any size will work. But, if you really rock it out and apply for a LOT of scholarships (as I hope you will) and your binder gets full, you can easily transfer these items to a larger binder.

- My <u>custom tracker</u>, to organize and keep track of all college and scholarship applications. This tracker will allow you to have everything in one place.

- A <u>thumb drive</u> to save your essay and letters of recommendations. This is needed for applications that require you to upload documents. Also, the thumb drive is a safe place to keep all your documents for easy access.

- Your <u>essay</u>. Rule of thumb is to ALWAYS have a general essay ready at ALL TIMES. Print 3 copies and place it in the binder. Don't forget to add your name, date and the name of the scholarship at the top!

- <u>Letters of recommendation</u>. Have at least 3 copies of each.
  If possible, have the writer to type it on their letterhead. A letterhead portrays professionalism and is more likely to be considered as legitimate by the reader.

  If they don't have a professional letterhead, ensure that they list their contact information at the top in a professional format. The key is appearance.

- <u>Envelopes and stamps</u>. Always have a handful of letter and document sized envelopes in your binder. While most applications are electronic, there are some organizations that still prefer a paper application. Having envelopes and stamps on hand will save you a lot of time and eliminate last minute trips to the post office.

- <u>Transcripts</u>. Request 3 copies of your official transcript from your guidance counselor. You'll find that majority of scholarships will require a transcript.

Tip: Request your transcripts early and often. Most schools have a 2-3 day period before they fill transcript requests, therefore it's important to request them early. Also, if you're applying for a lot of scholarships, you'll need plenty!

- <u>Resume</u>. You'll absolutely want to have several copies of your resume/ profile on hand. This is a list of all your accomplishments, awards and community service.

As I mentioned in an earlier chapter, your resume/ profile is YOUR opportunity to boast and showcase all of YOUR accomplishments!!

- <u>Labels</u>. Now this is a time-saver! With the volume of applications, I anticipate you'll be submitting, having a sheet of labels with your name and address increases efficiency and reduces finger cramps!

- <u>Pen and blank paper</u>. These items may seem minor, but they are essential. For example, my friends knew I was looking for scholarships; therefore, when they found one and called me with the details, I needed that pen and paper!

All information included in this book is based on my personal experience. Your experience and results may vary. I do not guarantee any college admissions nor scholarship awards.

NOTES

"To Do" Lists by Grade

Below is a list of recommended tasks for grades 9-12. This list is not all inclusive and should be used as a guide. Be sure to check with your high school and/or guidance counselor for any additional tasks.

Ninth Grade:

- Volunteer, volunteer, volunteer! Ninth grade is a great time to build your community service resume and accumulate hours.

- During the summer, consider getting a job and/or participate in enrichment camps. These are opportunities to build leadership skills.

- Complete a career assessment to see which jobs align with your interests.

- Your ninth-grade courses will appear on the transcript you send to colleges. Therefore, discuss taking any Advanced Placement and/or Honors courses with your guidance counselor.

Tenth Grade:

- Continue to stay involved in extracurricular activities. Keep volunteering and building your community service hours.

    Don't slack on your grades. Keep your grade point average as high as possible. It's easy for your GPA to drop, but it requires much more effort to increase it.

- Take the SAT and/or ACT, to get a feel for each test. This is great preparation for your junior year, when you'll take these tests more often.

- Begin building a relationship with your guidance counselor. Share you career aspirations and colleges you're interested in. Your counselor can connect you with individuals in his/ her network that can share insight about their careers or college experience.

Eleventh Grade:

- Register for the SAT and/or ACT tests and take them often, to get the highest score possible.

- Stay connected with your guidance counselor to ensure you're taking the required courses to satisfy all graduation requirements.

- Make a list of prospective colleges and contact them for information.

- Visit colleges and tour their campuses. If you can't visit in person, take a virtual tour online.

- Large college fairs are typically held around the country with hundreds of colleges in attendance. Search the web for when a fair will be in your area.

- Consider getting a summer job. Along with senior year comes fees, graduation pictures, etc. The extra money will help cover expenses and the experience will look great on your resume!

Twelfth Grade:

- When the FAFSA opens, be sure to complete it as early as possible. Colleges use this data to determine the amount of financial aid you'll receive.

- You should have a solid list of schools to which you want to apply. Submit your applications before the deadline. Remember, each school will have their own due dates. Add these dates to the tracker.

- If you're not satisfied with your SAT or ACT score, retake the tests in an attempt to increase your scores.

- Ensure that any transcripts, letters of recommendation or other information is submitted on time. This is a busy time for 12th grade counselors and they receive MANY requests.

- When acceptance letters begin to arrive, carefully evaluate each offer, don't rush. It's important to be 100% comfortable with your decision.

- Last but not least, CELEBRATE, you've made it to the 12th grade!!

NOTES

NOTES

Resources

As a <u>BONUS</u> for purchasing this book, I'd like to send you a tool kit which includes a prospective college checklist, college application tracker, scholarship tracker and a student resume template! Send an email to info@collegandscholarshiphelp.com and put TOOLKIT in the subject line.

I encourage you to utilize these tools during the college application and scholarship process. They were extremely beneficial for myself and others who have used them. Remember, there are MANY tasks associated with this process. Therefore, fully utilize ALL of the help you can!

To schedule a consultation, group workshop/ webinar or speaking opportunity, email your request to info@collegeandscholarshiphelp.com

Follow me on the following social media platforms, where I share scholarships, announce free webinars such as Chats with Admissions Advisors, Financial Aid Advisors and others.

Facebook:
https://facebook.com/collegeandscholarshiphelpjacksonville/
Twitter: https://twitter.com/candshelp/
Instagram: https://www.instagram.com/candshelp/

NOTES

<u>Acknowledgements</u>

Wanting to help others has always been my passion. Whether it's serving a meal to a needy family in my community or helping a first-generation college student and their parent navigate the college application and scholarship process.

Helping the next generation pursue their dream of attending college is much more fulfilling than any words can express.

Having the support of my family means a LOT. Therefore, I would like to sincerely thank my husband and children for their unwavering support!

Thank you to every College Admissions Advisor, Financial Aid Advisor, Guidance Counselor, High School teacher, family and friends who provided advice, insight and proofread a chapter. I appreciate you!

I'm often asked, "How do you manage to stay involved and help so many people and organizations?" My response is always, "It takes a LOT of calendar coordination and prioritizing." I'm simply serving others and demonstrating a Servant's heart.

I want to give a special THANKS to my eldest child, Shilah. Because of her desire to attend college, this served as the catalyst of what is now...College and Scholarship Help (The Planner LLC).

All of the information I researched, the resources I discovered and the lessons I learned all started with her college journey. Securing <u>over</u> $30,000 in scholarships and not having to pay any tuition costs was because of her willingness to stay the course, write MANY essays, submit MANY applications, research MANY websites and the list goes on and on.

Shilah I dedicate this book to YOU!

Made in the USA
Coppell, TX
24 May 2021